FROM **FLOWER** TO **HONEY**

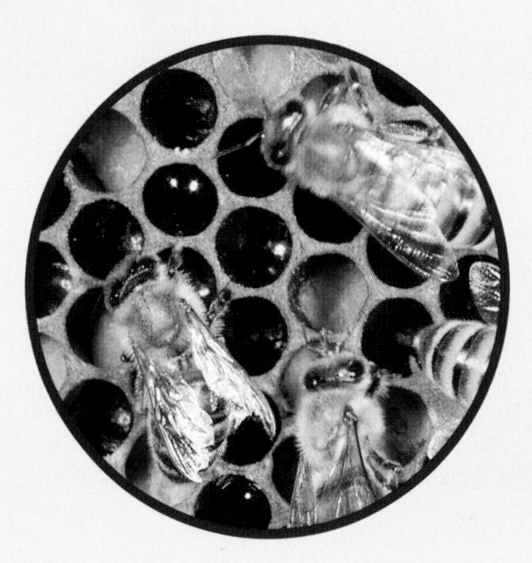

by Robin Nelson

Lerner Publications Company / Minneapolis

Lerner Publications Company
A division of Lerner Publishing Group
241 First Avenue North
Minneapolis, MN 55401 U.S.A.

Website address: www.lernerbooks.com

Library of Congress Cataloging-in-Publication Data

Nelson, Robin, 1971–
From flower to honey / by Robin Nelson.
p. cm. — (Start to finish)
Summary: Describes the process of making honey, from a bee's collection of nectar to honey production on a beekeeper's farm.
ISBN: 0–8225–0717–X (lib bdg. : alk. paper)
1. Honeybee—Juvenile literature. 2. Honey—Juvenile literature. 3. Bee culture—Juvenile literature.
[1. Honeybee. 2. Bees. 3. Honey. 4. Bee culture.]
I. Title. II. Start to finish (Minneapolis, Minn.)
SF523.5 .N46 2003
638'.1—dc21 2001005487

Manufactured in the United States of America
2 3 4 5 6 – JR – 08 07 06 05 04 03

The photographs in this book appear courtesy of: © Robert and Linda Mitchell, cover, pp. 1 (bottom), 9, 11, 13; © Karlene Schwartz, pp. 1 (top), 5; The National Honey Board, p. 3; © Dwight R. Kuhn, p. 7; Washington Apple Commission, p. 15; Draper's Super Bee Apiaries, Inc. www.draperbee.com, p. 17; Corbis Royalty Free Images, p. 19; © Beth Osthoff/Independent Picture Service, p. 21; © Lynda Richardson/CORBIS, p. 23.

Table of Contents

Honey is a sweet treat.

How is it made?

Flowers open.

Flowers start to open up each spring. There is a sweet juice called **nectar** inside each flower.

Bees fly to the flowers.

Bees fly from flower to flower.
They are looking for nectar.

Bees drink nectar.

Bees have a tongue that is like a straw. They suck up nectar with their long tongues.

Bees fly home.

The bees take the nectar to their home. A bee's home is its **hive**. The bees pass the nectar to other bees inside the hive. The wooden hives in this picture were built by people.

Bees store the nectar.

The bees put the nectar into a **honeycomb**. The honeycomb is made of wax. It has many holes in it. Bees fill each hole with nectar. The nectar dries. It turns into honey.

A beekeeper takes the honeycomb.

A **beekeeper** is a person who raises bees for honey. The beekeeper takes the honeycomb out of the hive. A beekeeper wears special clothing. The clothing protects the beekeeper from bee stings.

The beekeeper removes the honey.

The beekeeper puts the honeycomb into a machine that spins. The spinning squeezes the honey out of the honeycomb.

The beekeeper puts the honey in jars.

The beekeeper drains the honey to remove bits of honeycomb. Then the honey is poured into jars.

The honey is sent to stores.

Workers load the honey onto a truck. The truck takes the honey to grocery stores. People buy the honey and take it home.

Price Cut!
2.45
SMUCKER'S
Apple Jelly
Jif
CREAMY
SKIPPY
Welch's
Grape Jam
41800
24163
27087
Price Cut!
1.29
REDUCED FAT

Time to eat!

The honey is ready to eat. Honey makes food taste sweet. It even tastes good all by itself!

Glossary

beekeeper (BEE-kee-pur): a person who raises bees for their honey

hive (HYV): a home for bees

honeycomb (HUH-nee-kohm): a wax container with many holes that bees fill with nectar

nectar (NEK-tur): sweet juice that bees collect from flowers

Index